THE POETRY OF DUBNIUM

The Poetry of Dubnium

Walter the Educator

Silent King Books

SILENT KING BOOKS

SKB

Copyright © 2024 by Walter the Educator

All rights reserved. No part of this book may be reproduced in any manner whatsoever without written permission except in the case of brief quotations embodied in critical articles and reviews.

First Printing, 2024

Disclaimer
This book is a literary work; poems are not about specific persons, locations, situations, and/or circumstances unless mentioned in a historical context. This book is for entertainment and informational purposes only. The author and publisher offer this information without warranties expressed or implied. No matter the grounds, neither the author nor the publisher will be accountable for any losses, injuries, or other damages caused by the reader's use of this book. The use of this book acknowledges an understanding and acceptance of this disclaimer.

"Earning a degree in chemistry changed my life!"
— Walter the Educator

dedicated to all the chemistry lovers, like myself, across the world

DUBNIUM

Dubnium stands tall

DUBNIUM

A symbol of scientific wonder, never to fall

DUBNIUM

With atomic number one hundred and five

DUBNIUM

It's a marvel of the periodic table, so alive

DUBNIUM

Discovered in labs, through ingenious means

DUBNIUM

Dubnium's existence, a triumph, it gleams

DUBNIUM

Synthesized with care, by skilled hands

DUBNIUM

A testament to human curiosity, that expands

DUBNIUM

Its properties, mysterious and rare

DUBNIUM

Unraveling its secrets, takes utmost care

DUBNIUM

A fleeting existence, in the atomic dance

DUBNIUM

Dubnium's nature, a scientific romance

DUBNIUM

In the depths of the atom, it holds its sway

DUBNIUM

A fleeting glimpse, before it fades away

DUBNIUM

Its isotopes, fleeting and unstable

DUBNIUM

Yet in their study, we find a fable

DUBNIUM

Dubnium, a name that echoes through time

DUBNIUM

A testament to human intellect, so sublime

DUBNIUM

In the grand tapestry of the elements' dance

DUBNIUM

Dubnium's presence, a fleeting chance

DUBNIUM

Its electrons, in a delicate balance

DUBNIUM

A dance of energy, a cosmic trance

DUBNIUM

The nucleus, a realm of protons and neutrons

DUBNIUM

Dubnium's domain, where science adjourns

DUBNIUM

In laboratories, where minds collide

DUBNIUM

Dubnium's nature, they tirelessly tried

DUBNIUM

To understand its essence, its atomic soul

DUBNIUM

A quest for knowledge, an eternal goal

DUBNIUM

In the universe's grand atomic symphony

DUBNIUM

Dubnium plays a part, in its cosmic harmony

DUBNIUM

A piece of the puzzle, in the grand design

DUBNIUM

A testament to human intellect, so divine

DUBNIUM

So here's to Dubnium, in all its glory

DUBNIUM

A symbol of human scientific story

DUBNIUM

In the grand saga of the elements' tale

DUBNIUM

Dubnium's presence, we'll forever hail

DUBNIUM

In the cosmic cauldron, where stars are born

DUBNIUM

Dubnium's secrets, are waiting to be adorned

DUBNIUM

A shimmering enigma, in the atomic dance

DUBNIUM

A puzzle piece, in the universe's expanse

DUBNIUM

ABOUT THE CREATOR

Walter the Educator is one of the pseudonyms for Walter Anderson. Formally educated in Chemistry, Business, and Education, he is an educator, an author, a diverse entrepreneur, and he is the son of a disabled war veteran. "Walter the Educator" shares his time between educating and creating. He holds interests and owns several creative projects that entertain, enlighten, enhance, and educate, hoping to inspire and motivate you.

Follow, find new works, and stay up to date
with Walter the Educator™
at WaltertheEducator.com

www.ingramcontent.com/pod-product-compliance
Lightning Source LLC
LaVergne TN
LVHW051921060526
838201LV00060B/4108